RAPPORT
PRIVILEGE

Poems by Creed J. Shepard

Kansas City   Spartan Press   Missouri

Spartan Press
Kansas City, Missouri
spartanpresskc.com

Spartan Press

Copyright (c) Creed J. Shepard 2017
First Edition 1 3 5 7 9 10 8 6 4 2
ISBN: 978-1-946642-04-2
LCC#: 2017930856

Design, edits and layout: Jason Ryberg
Author photo: Jamie Hofling
Cover painting: Gregory Thomas (gregariousarts.weebly.com)
All rights reserved. No part of this publication may be
reproduced or transmitted in any form or by any means,
electronic or mechanical, including photocopying,
recording or by info retrieval system, without prior
written permission from the author.

ACKNOWLEDGMENTS

Spartan Press would like to thank Prospero's Books, Jeanette Powers, j.d.tulloch, Jason Preu, Mark McClane, Tony Hayden and the Osage Arts Community.

From the author:

Much like my third chapbook, *Rapport Privilege,* this fourth chapbook, *Rapport Privilege,* is dedicated to my family, all those familiar but somehow mysterious sources of inspiration. To be sure the violence in this *work* comes from elsewhere. On that note, remember to read once, then re-read slowly.

These poems were written and/or constructed between 2014-2016. Most of the first section of *Stanzas Contra The Construct of Childhood* was a stanza by stanza interaction with Kim Addonizio's poem, *Scary Movies*

All The Sounds   Together Fine is a plundering of Tony Mancus's *All The Sounds Run Together Fine,* with which I employ a variation of one of Bernadette Mayer's Writing Experiments, which can be found at http://writing.upenn.edu/library/Mayer-Bernadette_Experiments.html. *All The Sounds Runs Together Fine* was published in the Summer, 2014 issue of Sixth Finch.

Thanks to my friend, Taylor Ford for the *hot dogs.* Thanks to my ecstatically reliable lovely Jamie for her ears. A very special thanks to Jason Ryberg and Spartan Press for making this book possible. Thank you-all so much for reading this. Serious Love.

CONTENTS

Online Social Networking in Your Sleep / 1
Will You Forgive Me if I Still Have
    a Relationship with You In My Head? / 3
Catachresis Glut / 7
Hotdog Tenderness / 9
Speaking of Well Directed Rage / 10
I Don't Know Why Photo Albums
  Never Replaced Museums / 11
Speaking of Personalized Unassuming Monuments / 12
Sui Generis / 14
Stanzas in the Face of the Construct of Childhood / 16
Could've Would've Didn't / 20
Rapport Privilege / 21
Constituency Fishing (Yes, Again) / 26
Favorite Serenade / 27
Is It Alright in the Air at Night? / 29
Long Moment / 31
Her First Word / 33
Conspicuously Safe / 34
Speaking of Threatened Park Animals / 40
Slut Talk Instructions to Surviving the Wreck / 46
Foreign Youth Ambassadors / 51
Harpo's Veritable Forest / 53
Post Pre-Rapport / 55
Rapport Reprise / 59
All the Sounds   Together Fine / 60

I put society at odds with a family,
letting a new sound be again,
& I send a warm thing by a spoon over a slow one.

Again I discuss something brown.
& once again I'm willing myself dead of I'm coming to see
something narrow.

-Jackson Mac Low

We want to believe that what we are in relation to
is unique.

-Jackie Clark

Online Social Networking in Your Sleep

Your keeping track of the
time is supposed to anchor.

But the rattle of Greta's purr

at the comfy chair in the room
Where the neighbor sometimes peeps in

Friends fake ask me,
Lara, you use the adverb, "aesthetically"
a lot, and I respond,
why yes, it is a weighty category
in my mind and I mind

it when some
thing so full of content doesn't
move me. Something
so full of contentment.

Our skins are tickled with echoes
of Greta's meow
that is like the sausage
of a caress
It doesn't have to be fancy
a little wet, yes

Admittedly the feeling out of a rigid shape
punctuates the trill purr
or a hope for social change
in some correlative relation to log-offs

A document of
expression, obsess over its palimpsest.

It's not that I need a Jewel weed
to send ringtones of Terry Riley
out its stamen
or porn scenes of biggest professor crushes
or resented fellow students

But this lack of an end to a time line
The impressions of some awful
request in writing that is impossible
from the other end of your eyes

Will You Forgive Me if I Still Have a Relationship with You in My Head?

This one person? What is
their connection to the world
They think they can just look
at some object,
crab apple tree out front, or what's for dinner

and warmly hug with words:
This

and feel satisfied.

This time they pull up their skirt
just to touch their innermost thighs
to tell if it will touch back?

Etiolated rubber letters on the Enter Button
of the remote control

A clumsy fool, I don't deserve what I have.
Expatiation: a personal connection to the world

Bach's passacaglia and fugue in C
minor
du Bouchet's figure of speech fast

escape while you can from this

                    Not the world, no, jeez!
From this portrait of this one person

The first person
the first person and not in first person

turn the page
I prepare for Jamie's coming
home. My home our home and yet
they, so many of them live in our minds
apparitions which do not
need forms
To shape an exact
visceral state type.

Bend over or go backwards
an ear to the speaker
to feel what is meant

A precise scoff
reaches a third party
You mistook my hand
for an extension
of your spasms

And having the nerve
to ask me
if I'm sure
I'm not lying to myself

Scoffing salvaged for you
and the third party
Who plots --mum-- destruction
as well.

It's Afternoon in America
Too white for the white &
black kids, the sprinkler
system manager
could tell
his ears, the intended
recipients.

Hagh ghah uhah
I can't picture any body
part as I use it
hagh, ghah uhah
empathic presence
as an absent minded
pervert

I am afraid of people
because I hate lack of intimacy. With more subtlety:
impatient

*

that he waited to feel as one until everyone else
passed the coffin just to even kiss her
that he waited to feel as one that it was impossible.

Just to even kiss her seemed impossible.

After his newlywed wife's death, at the longish moment of his pain, weaving in and out, up and down, and through his chest cavity, he remembered making the thought: *at*
some point I'll have to choose whether to shut down
and not be open to anyone again…

*

Horror(ible) Story Lessons:
White guilt is elemental
but brown shit is permanental

You're biologically
wired
to pay attention to that sound

The density of the snarl
is not known

to have any particular bounds

Words with strong first and second consonants
like *for*
and *give* to (")start(")

Satisfy this hungriness
Let the wind blow through your heart

Catachresis Glut

Think the most titillating yet detailed blueprints of
real affection.
But that's just shop talk,
the maker too smug to share them with the buyers,
and assuming
buyer's rejoice

Determining them to be fully jaded

Wasn't even a story line
except to ask the cute server
to stop frowning, to ask her

to stop suspecting my eyes
a pair of violent sex pots
with hairy spiked penises
at the center of their pupils

The center that is the effect
of the eyes meeting
the center not seen
to confess it's our target

Eyes, always each other's
target--not meaning, just our looking
perhaps a shield
an edging border

At the border of...the spine of
their reluctant approach

Instead –yes I mean instead,
as a nautical tree vase
shaped just for some evolutionary
reimagining of the ear
The ear of the recompense
husks husks out
Excuses for awkwardness

Sea shells that mouth
Margins at the curl

embracing bodily friend
mistaken for void
forgetting to tell each other how we feel

in the decisive public pivot
pockets of the rocky ground
catch feet from falling

Hotdog Tenderness

Nobody wants to be the guy who eats the last
hot dog.
And that it's a female who inquires as to if there are
any more hot dogs
I feel some shame that I took the last hot dog

Here I am. Another man, robbing her of the
experience of eating the hotdog
Did I know that it was the last hot dog?
Should I have known that it was the last hot
dog?

I winced when the other man, manning the grill,
announced to her they were out of hot dogs

I felt so bad I walked far away
to eat the second half of my hotdog

Speaking of Well Directed Rage

If it was a poor black person
applying, he wouldn't be eligible
either,
no sir

We don't have opinions here at the Marketplace
I have interpreted your question as abusive,
sir, could you — because I know how good you
are with hypotheticals —
plausibly see that taken offense is so obvious, if
also, as you say, extreme

You are not eligible for an affordable health care
plan because, again,
your state is not expanding Medicaid to cover
single individuals
at your income level
and you do not make enough for the tax credit to
lower the cost of a Federally Facilitated
Marketplace Health plan.

If you would like to be a black person you can
take my place on the call and I can transfer you
to my supervisor
Yes sir, good luck to you

I Don't Know Why Photo Albums Never Replaced Museums

Speaking of well-directed rage,
where it hurts the most,
along someone else's monuments
The implicit rejection by their
cis forefathers' greatest accomplishments
whose art thoughtfully challenges
history, almost everyone's
But his legs keep on, as if driven, yet
he will not stop for this installation
art. Supposing no one needs a witness,
he doesn't remember when
great great great great great great
Grandpa May
had his bio-power robbed in some coal mine
in Mostyn for some just imaginable pittance, and
but still managed to spawn an heir,
his great great great great great Grandpa May
The *unus mundus's* impossibility
goes without saying for that's when they
went to the new world,
never wearing black on their faces again
Probably

Speaking Of Personalized Unassuming Monuments

The enjambment of this neighborhood the
pedestrian is always ensconced in
stammering everyday when trying not
to alienate you.
When metaphors are so
new it won't develop,

why the line stops right on nineteenth street
mobile homes ornamented with barking dogs
then continues.

It's the same way with new
transportation infrastructure
Being on foot with your bike until carrying
over the railing the tire-friendly pavement
wouldn't be possible without
the old way cities like Lawrence still
create economic growth. Parents always
lashing that one should not complain
about the bringers by
whom our favorite shows
were brought to us

Tire-friendly pavement
on the long road through the
teasingly pastoral

corridor—teasing because it'll be gone soon
and—the point reached, trying
to be made is: the only thing
more place-making than an urban landscape
where free from any and all commerce

is the toy store
that is Nu Penny on the other end
of that dead end
just north
of the still concealingly electrifying pylons

Sui Generis

The ones who loved us best are the ones we'll lay to rest...
The ones who love us least are the ones we'll die to please

— Paul Westerberg

It hurts not knowing how I got here; of course
that's one of my figures of speech.
That helps describe what makes me want to
reconcile with those
who would keep me down
with those who'd still keep me down

Now is a good time amid the charges of my
arrogance
to talk about the time I wet my pants.
I still wet the bed

I'll never be smarter
I'll never be stronger than now
[this is where the reverb is laid on thick]
And while I learned to love you
better than average

Inside this embodied mind secrets are kept
even from me
Writing poetry exposes *radical subjectivity*
Radical Subjectivity
Radical Subjectivity
Radical Subjectivity

And the euphoric effects of an enthused but
threatened
freedom. Freedom
Oh, freedom.

There is sorrow knowing that we
rely on those who don't love us
We depend on some who don't love us
We need many who do not know us.

The sorrow knowing that
what's wrong with the system is above our pay
grade
What's wrong with the system
is
above our pay grade
What's wrong with
the system is above our pay grade
What's wrong
with the system is above our pay grade

Stanzas in the Face of the Construct of Childhood

For example the primal feeling,
somewhat common
fear of getting pregnant,
the belief that almost anything can get a girl
pregnant

The children invent parts of horror stories to
make up for the things they know they're kept
from knowing. Then when they discover all
those things adults kept from them, they forget
to compare to see if their inventions are scarier
than—than, well, golly what in the world

Cotton Balls bleed out the sides of their
fanged mouths, a perfect discouragement
surely leading to difficult thoughts
starring James Craig Gloria Talbot

Lon Chaney Tom Drake daring to challenge
the unknown, the world of the Cyclops
But I won't have to do the dishes
Troglodytes shake sparklers taunting: *you're stuck!*

Nowadays not even a whisper
lives next door to reproductive organs
let alone a cry of *Shilo, when I was young*

As a young child at the movies meant
to entertain while the adults in my
real life, at noon, don't exist
The cannibalistic crib of the Cyclops—

Don't argue, I know what human bones look
like, and I can smell them over brothers'
B.O., the popcorn and the hard candies
That's what depression is like, doing nothing.

Laziness truly is another agent
as real as parents or bullies
I mean free will is debatable but
distancing myself from addicted cousin

Because he will drag me down with
him next to the cleaned but cigarette-
stained yellow bones, near death, undead
Or the friend in the same situation

who already turned down your offer
of dinner and a day at the park.
We were both there at mutual
loved one's funeral. For him not a day for friends

Not individual, specific friends
Certainly a lively—an active cave
to be wandering in after learning
escape possible, but requiring

getting in that Vampire cloud's face
But it reminds too much of cauliflower
in a garden ruled by the lord of
nightmares, The Cyclops!
If I so much as open my mouth
a cyclops turd will fly in
a poison cyclops turd. But then,
parents would turn on the lights

and pull the sheets off
including the ones tacked to the
chair making a fort in the corner,
about to show what it feels like

*

At the shooting range
now seeing
with clarity and distance
the would-be reparations
(even) Ne was robbed of any opportunity
to be born alone
to figure it out for
nemself
Some way to learn affection
under a knife and sterile lights

*

They called him *Bic*
like the shaving razor
because at fifteen he hadn't
gone through puberty

Half-life
if only memory
was that long
I plan to invent a girlhood

What congregates at crowded buildings
that doesn't have a pulse
or serial numbers. But
they aren't your daddy's boom booms

Even among the readers
people love explosions
and all kinds of storms
Ooh, and *ahs,* failed the onomatopoeia

Life for most goes on for a bit
We be watching the triple fruit
line up and where's the broken bucket
Fuck it, I am not of the en-Vie-Earn-ment

Could've Would've Didn't

On Abelism, maybe.
Liminal parsing of the
ability and the willingness
to hear:
If I had
screamed
bicycle on your left!
while coming from behind
wouldn't it have been rude?
the wind was coming
from the north that
day, the direction we were
all heading. Yes mam,
obviously, you *didn't hear me*
obviously ability
should not have been
assumed—I won't
bring my soar throat
into it. The ambulance
has four wheels my
bike has two, you
are still on two walking legs
sorry your husband
grabbed your body
and held it so close to him

Rapport Privilege

To try to share the dilettante's experience
Some have even credited it with
replacing museums—logically
Logically?
These homely drawings, poems and songs
Embracing everyone within the privacy of

Homely is a euphemism for retarded
Itself an epithet for intellectually disabled
But we mean homely in the way that
many intellectually disabled people
look absolutely beautiful and some
intellectually enabled people look beautiful only
in the way we think intellectually disabled people
do
Abandoning the footnotes of transgressions

What a path to take, is it a shameless conceit or
some kind of undiagnosed mental illness
What a path to devise:
thinking outside the box requires a
literal cardboard box to advertise the support of
unalienated labor
Playing with the idea that Adam was a mere first
dénoter, three dollars
playing with it *a capella,* five dollars

So resentment takes its steps toward oblivion
and wounds from the dictatorship of capital
gently exits, is not a cliché
for a more exciting rugged individualism that
permeates through the streets, is a cliché
The word cliché not much of one, merely
a necessary first step
to begin conversation   now stick your
salacious head back in your hearth tent,
conversation. Not
subjectifying you today, conversation
no no no! no no no noeoah!

An indirect benediction in this, a result of the
lack of conversation

Then there's this nonconsensual sex the boys
and girls have at the school
Nonconsensual sex is a euphemism for rape
We, who only witnessed the testimonies, our
straight men's mouths, no longer open wide,
mildly filtering the salutary growls
prototypically erecting an inept transformation
from her victimhood
to some fetishized demystification of the
rapist in all his hygiene challenged chat room
isolation
        He without meaningful rapport, with
nothing. Nothing without
the habitual propulsion to assert a fixed
subjectivity

that dreams a collective maker of his victimhood
that meets a salutary growl and probably
weaponry

You'll see how *we are* the kneecap
of the joke
Our mouth wants to open wide and mildly filter
the salutary growl
As for we who have rapport privilege…

They say Rapport Privilege
rules a nation, or a
mass of … or the one or two dozen lines
that'll manage to survive its decay,
you can tell
one's accentuating of tits, ass, hips and the
color pink cannot remain a concept alone. At
best a means
to liberate for real

Even Whitman's Scud is improved
by that scuff mark
which never showing
what *fremdschämen* the
friendship substitution canonization might
include,
Why are the blurbs all written by the author's friends?
Why have I never been published outside Kansas?

Surely more than just overreaching
send-ups to the overrated *Howl*
that standing list of
quasi-innumerable incidents with friends,
involving bodily
positions/situations in important public places
prepositionally referencing something
phony/mystical in the faces of oppression, amid
mid-century American culture

Just what is this thing
called the hipster millennial set
it is not like we count their numbers
in a non inept political war room
once it's left *your head it's already
compromised*
But let's keep going…on a fluke, one
of many that season, he
can't say he *suffers* from
rapport privilege
but then not *suffer* from white,
male privilege either

*This Rapport Privilege is a lie. I have never
cashed in on my Rapport privilege*

*If you study the history of Rapport Privilege our
ship captains were getting murdered. The
French had to tip us off. I mean these were the
days of Thomas Jefferson…you can't solve it with dia-*

*logue. You can't solve it with a summit.
You solve it with a bullet to the head. It's the
only thing these people understand. And
all we've heard from this President is a case to
heap praise on Rapport Privilege, as if to
appease them.*

*It's clear that Rapport Privilege is a threat to the world.
Yet, President Obama will not say that*

Oooohhh oooohhhh, not subjectifying you to
oday, conversation.

Constituency Fishing (Yes, Again)

How many times does it take
for the same characteristic
of a thing to lead one to believe
that that characteristic is
is an essential part of the thing.

44 men and now Hillary.

On the other hand
there are only two—

(the) perpetual war(s):

There being numerations
for things
that we honestly feel
are *innumerable*

Will you stand up to be counted?
At least within the
first 310 million

I kind of mean this: Prayer:
that the antipathies and empathies
projected onto media protagonists
come back to us to each other, unAlt-Washable
like the highest avant-garde poem

Favorite Serenade

I know you won't think this is a favorite serenade
of mine,
my one free arm achingly trying to engage—the
fighting as
a means only, to reach the most neutral zone of
communication

The most neutral zone of communication

Thinking you have to earn privilege of talking
about abstract things.

Toddler Leo stands holding the squeeze box
accordion
looking and intently fishing-for, at
baby brother Otto in his baby seat

Not everyone can love
words as much as you
Not everyone gets that certain phrases can be
lovable tautologies
like: land bridge, Cola Beverage, conceptual art
object or squeeze box accordion

Like saying you really have to earn
the privilege of conversing
about abstract things, toddler
Leo stands holding the accordion

Like managing to explain why the explanation of
the multiple global crises is relevant to the house
she and her husband will build, Jill decides to
keep up with his new friend up ahead at the foot
of the rocky bluff by asking for someone to save
his bicycle she's holding with her left arm while
using her right to hold onto the rocky ledge. It is
very dark with only a few seemingly random
traffic lights and there is much ground to cover
before reaching their destination. She feels so
light—we all do when traveling. Exclusively
local diets are not yet feared

Like some admission of guilt for having dropped
something,
the neutral zone of communication is the slow
sculpture of a human face that is always
improving, always looking ahead

Like the man condemned and awarded to live
with the talking finger, toddler Leo spends a lot
of time offering expressions of love to baby
brother Otto

Will Leo even know the intensity and
amortization of that expense? Does anyone?

Is it Alright in the Air at Night?

Those people? In Manhattan? They are better than us, because they want things they haven't seen.
>-Peggy Olson as written by Tom Palmer
> and Matther Weiner

We assume understanding and are obliged to roll our eyes, reintroducing calamity to that which instigates.
>-Jackie Clark

Later the sophistication
they acquired
would stifle them

Can't do any better
than message in bottle

The song settles inside
the body it borrows

Lullabies become unrecognizable
in pleasant forms
Still, oceanic experiences happen
The stubborn unclosed loop shows
faith in the other, even if in The Other

Whereas, on the more adaptable land,
acquaintanceship is instrumental,
      maybe key

there will be no resistance to
the speed of content exchange
registering monologues of acronyms

Sing with your child on your back or front
in front of a very enthusiastic crowd in the dark

And where is the light?

Long Moment

The sound of money is very quiet indeed
And there is Boketto
The simplest and most explicit
tally criterion on the
Bohemian index.

That is a thing
Guest lists of shared hopes and values
are not the X factor?
The thing will insulate us from

noise, the business world
anything dubbed *enhanced*
Then pink lines and pink drills
across the land
Making this observation,
and yet I am Peter Pan,
euphemism for not outside of loser spectrum
fallen back in terror for myself, for
placebo conversations that must catch on.
My life still synecdoche for
body of rash and fatigue

But there is Boketto
and it potentially affects over the whole brain
till a series of movements is only recognized as
a whole state

Ronald Reagan was ridiculed as an actor
an actor without a moment
nevertheless influential friends and party members
persevered

I can't believe I'm loved by you this much Jamie
ccnntt bbllvv mm llvvdd bb yy thths mmchch jjmm
I can't believe I'm loved by you this much Jamie
ccnntt bbllvv mm llvvdd bb yy thths mmchch jjmm
Aye-a-ee-ee-aye-uh-aye-oo-i-uh-ay-ee
Aye-a-ee-ee-aye-uh-aye-oo i-uh-ay-ee

Her First Word

      Her first word was baby
          Pretty soon everyone was a baby
            to the point of the TV
      almost falling off the table
    in the narrow crook by
      the bed
  I taught her, so I'd like to think,
      how to clap her hands
        to the point where I
        forgot she was
      the force of nature

Emile crawled an authorship
      of how many meters today?

*

New York Mayoral race 2013: Anthony
Weiner's protagonism
    The media makes a New York   just
for courtin'
      And what it means to have hands
          of one's own
  is erased by someone else's happiness
        someone else's precious
      but repeatable joy

and three dogs   Alaskan Malamute
perhaps with a little Belgian Malinois in her   or
Dutch or German
Shepard – close enough to wild wolves around
this babe

Conspicuously Safe

1. "-LATION" IN THE VIOLATION

The other hour
while saying we gotta heal out divisions

>   the Camel Cricket
>   The Camel Cricket
>   shimmied out the
>   middle passage of my beard
>   Unbeknownst to me

and in that hour
      we verbally acknowledged the vision
in the Trump rally bleechers—the audience
remembering the man's sucker shock elbow
      to the face of his *big mouth*
the black protestor walking up the stairs
      green twigs of a noble gray
      I'm sorry I lost my place in this
hour.

If he comes back we may have to kill him
      I lost my place in this hour
      and the Camel Cricket still shimmied
      through the seemingly kept bramble
      going to something to eat on
      and—as the letters still arrive to the
      Electors—
My beard's witness speaks to, not for it

Now, in the least hurry
          months after the incident
with   unsupervised probation for   one year

the white man and his elbowed big mouth hug
each other.

          feeling conspicuously safe
                    and
          a self-evident love
          awaits our tiny violations us, straight
white men

          to each other
conspicuously less auspicious
          feeling for confrontation
I scuttle
          good smells
                    when we cuddle, my beard
hides formerly wheezed good smells almost
          almost the thing to keep poised

2. PROFESSIONAL PROLETARIAN AFTER
   TRUMP

          Conspicuously safe

                    undeservingly (?)

Who wants some
ice cream!

And Bent Star Scum
    the dishwasher's regal eye(s)
        absolves the drain

watching the trachea
    amplify the smallest unit

too cold to care
    about anything but staying warm

walking alone, if you think,
   who will notice
You'll—I would anyway—
   refocus
on Bent Star Scum:
what day is it? What week what month
   what year!
To deserve eponymously
    attended commemoration

  the paradigm—no, standard shift in the
mid twenty-tens

    Frank Capra films attractive
      all the sudden!

        Neruda's paternalistic Odes,
            maybe can get through them now

            Meanwhile!
              Meanwhile the currency of in-person
conversation
          rises
       at the least most least:
            an insider tip

    Time to eat
     more fat the fascist will have
      to get to cut you down.

3. TOUCH

        To cut you down
            like a nasty bitch
       multiply number of
           tweets in a day
     by joules per second.

I know, I know they say that the worst thing about
those there online social networks
    is us. But

        I simply say, or can say
          that about anything
      say that about a boat out on a mission

—a boat that had to be designed
or at least
       built
say that about worn clothes
       that about money
       that about music

    So, to cut you down
  like a nasty bitch
      makes me wonder –and
  otherwise want to wonder—
  where else does that
    energy go without saying something
saying something   anything (!)
    to make the

    ballast cry out a watt
      just one watt – in the room
        a group of us underneath

    this is why I think
      you perfected listening
    through Bob Ross's painting lessons

    Still she thinks that people are essentially
good
      The light bulb existentially
    seasoned with ____

Luminosity Equals Meaning
Amplitude Equals Meaning
      As if
      As if
      As if   As if, period.
        The soft skin rises
like the cream, but different
    to be allowed that instant
      where touch
    (just that word touch!)
is the benign point of the blade

Speaking of Threatened Park Animals

...and two ugly stories why.
make your own choice; either could be.
Hearing, seeing, I believe both of them

-William Bronk

1.
My friend Gerald giving scruff of a neck
The right wisp of the cleaving of his lips

Amid his mantras we scrambled to feel the
anything-ascence once again

The way the cartoon dog mourns the loss
of her litter of puppies
crushed by a hoister's scoop while
she was out seeking ... formula?
The tragedy the neck has the pain threshold to
____m the dream

Not so tough myself, watching the time as a
coping
      mechanism   put   self in   place:
One rung above gullibility
while my dear friend Gerald betrays me—
        the anything-ascence again
     But this time, his.

     Finding myself ing-ing parts under the
hood
not just believing anything will fix it, but tinkering

2.
Anyway good ol' Soltera pandiculated almost
like a cat,
licked her chops and went back to
what we can only call mourning. Narratives are,
again,
a tyranny   implying a way of being

      that ignores the possibility of
conflict-free communication. That
      misunderstanding is necessary to
narratives
      Let the blue eyed equestrian Geralds
inside of you follow me

misunderstanding is necessary to—
misunderstanding is—misunderstanding—mis—
understanding is necessary to narratives—
understanding is necessary to—
standing is —necessary to narratives—
necessary to—necessary
necessary to narratives—to narratives—
narratives
-ary narratives—narrate—nar—
ratives wary are the natives

3.
that plot of *land*
the only thing in the world worth
fightin' for, worth dyin' for lasts.

Meanwhile he/it/they and yes, even she
surrounds us all!
Mantras bereft of resolution-seeking.

Therianthropic primer for an otherwise ambient
or airy plot

    Out of the *plain* without explaining
the old NVC the big man
needs violent car This dog hunts AND
has a good sense of boundaries
       and feels! the flexing pivot of the
       classic *meanwhile*

    This human ___s their territory,
    but too shook to crow

4.

There is that caterwaul again
    undecipherable of whether it is of joy or
sorrow Soltera and i have this in common
    too hungry to take advice. *A hungry
hungry horse,* added in the strongest Irish-
Confederate

accent, so my friend Gerald shared with me his
drink and dotty love vibrations.
    He has just enough memory to be my
friend Gerald.

My friend Gerald, she smells so good
        and at no time did her sad
                longing to connect impede
the less gracious attempt
     to turn meta her sad yarn from a prompt
to share
what could never last, if everyone else
   or every would-be mingler
              mattered too

5.
The author had a grandfather who drove a
hoister and belonged to a Hoister's Union
Author is guilty of a big mouth, has caused
others' discomfort because of it without the
intention to do so, not without a reasonable
doubt. Not the kinda things to tell just to get laid
right?

Riding out spouseless, childless, landless,
careerless just to tell

the delusion of some yippee ki-yay! southern
resurrection of a crueler animal

redeeming this yelp.

Soltera licked her chops then crouched back
onto the floor looking briefly at us with

those sad eyes, then furrowing her brow in some
other downward direction

Look! there's newly crushed Mittens, the biggest
pup of them. Soltera checked behind his ears for
worms that might have encouraged a once alive
Mittens a tender command to roll on his belly

That place with a pond and a shed nearby. But —
stupid— she has no memory for these kinds of
things

A manger or flat or whatever.

Solerta rubbed mittens's belly dry
till yelping towards a squirrel
which was really nowhere near a body
of water that wasn't safe to drink anyway

6.
Well, old buddy, Gerald conveyed, we just
remediated this celluloid lathe

If that's possible. I don't feel you, I told
him, though I understand your meaning. It's not what I
thought Post-Post-Internet Cinema would be
Am I quite incapable of rendering that machine
turnable That was not a question

Lips, quite flappable not clear at all with all this
pain in the neck that Mittens could often be to
Soltera. Not any kind of animal, but my friend
Gerald

        not afraid of change, what the
        human agency recasts
        to the frame   dark
like an orgasm   Conned, conversation
        friending this park to
disappear in   swift foot it's in the genes more
reasons to save Soltera
satisfied coz I know it'll love me
much the clay soil of their castle
spoiled ungulate grafts assle onto assle

And weary are those natives
having found [finally] something in common

Slut Talk Instructions to Surviving the Wreck

1. SLUT DISCLAIMER

A green light from his left turn on a red,
linger over the slowing down of time;
    note, no difference made
    to the state of her car dragged along
    by that drunk man's truck
Her factual statements mistaken by Officer X
    for apologies or excuses
    for all these failed reinvented tricks

The world being indifferent to that kind of
    experience
        And almost so towards The Walk

2. PURPOSE OF LESSON

Self-acknowledged exploiters of the touch
deprived,
    some say you could do worse
    and be underground working with rocks,
    breathing in their dust

3. ASSEMBLY

Now make it alluring.
> Done so when also repulsive
> or blinded by a gentleman-gazed periapt,
> those
> put-forth cascades from panty lines,
> stretch marks,
> down to a pinch of real stretched
> *gastrocnemii*

Look at it long enough to be helpful for witness account
> note, the privilege of such measured
> transparence
> when the limbs turn, stand still, twirl, jerk
> and/or break

Now, follow the officer's pen and
> walk the straight line
> Grapple with how natural and arbited
> holes could be the same
> as crisis mode is the primary mode to be
> in

Stay busy smiling that the meaning of sluts
> being challenged
> Even among depths of ignorance and/or
> instructor's aversion to self-esteem talk it's
> easy   to stay positive about this turn.
> This turn easily filled and cranking out
> the said periapts. Art Nouveau and its

       psychedelic rebirths gave us
       glimpes but it's still not clear

       what form that vulvic beacon will take

Stay positive, albeit even a gob of cum will not
    likely
    index to a fee schedule
    A gob of cum nor the quality of its
    generation will not replace
    nor even supplement time as reliable
    measure of price/value
    Like now is it too late to instruct
    attributions of agender
    to this authorship?

    irredeemable bromances,
    watch those beneficiary-benefactors

    of rapport privilege

4. DISCLAIMER II

Question asked sultry or smarmy accompanying furrowed brow: what is giving really?

What is the origin of that resentment from other women about the seeming ease with which you do what you do for a living, that for some of them is hard to enjoy for free?

5. INSTRUCTIONS

Have it recur in your head how bullying it gets,
> void of time with ovum or other relaxed
> scuttles

Go tell the policeman, who does not know what
> it's like to be a woman
> or any civilian intimidated by a policeman

after all—tell him we
> had our seat-belts on or other
> protections.

Tell him that your right-of-way was at the spot
> where
> we'd start walking, slutwise or otherwise,
> walking
> home anyway aspiring to melismatic
> shriek
> *—not obedient enough for you officer?—*
> before the good old boy's mockery has
> any effect

Turn, going around, trying to make happen,
> arouse
> turning right at the spot where
> walking is no longer some near
> disposable object of time,

Take aim, made facing hours of agony given to
> you
> and effortlessly hear the stories as the
> finest steel and glass tumbles

Note, what is called self hatred is incoherent in a

> troglodyte party you're not invited to
> Its slattern workings of hands burning
> effigies of the little groundlings,
> the men and women who praise them

Finally, good sport, make tangible blown kisses
> and a few catcalls and straight indirect
> sexual propositions
> embedded graphemes in the design of
> the vehicle, accommodating all levels of
> manly *vroom*.

And be sensitive! to the level of manly *vrroom*
> preceding any violated body
> For the national debate still rages outside
> of the body shop:
> is it rape culture, or automation
> that is to sex what Rapport Privilege is to
> intimacy?

Speak *Rape Culture* for
> hermeneutical bliss. Because less literal
> troglodytes need a party where there
> literally is no place to crash to start us
> coming statistically challenged
> statistically endangered, statistically-
> challenged;
> wall-picking its distinction from
> victimization
> The transliteration interrupted by by
> flotsam
> Abhorring the vacuous, your confused,
> however generous and humble instructor(s)
> reimagines a better *vroom*

Foreign Youth Ambassadors

Foreign Exchange Student
the sexiest
names that bring me back to the moment

Talking about those names

Parents together, am I
trippin'—
Most of them were from Mexico or Bulgaria

One night we were chillin, lookin'
at everybody's passports
and there was my mom
with her purse
Dad and her standing looking
pissed and embarrassed at
the same time

They look busted at the FYA dorm
*

I've always loved foreign exchange students

It seems so perfect
something so ironic about it
Not in the way I loved cats
or broccoli

My favorite Bulgarian
uh…there was an Albanian too—it
started with an *R*

What the fuck was he doing there
He gave me my first Zippo
Mom and dad were then still nostalgic for their
first post honey moon phase
*

Did you ever have a fascination with foreign
exchange students
they always had experiences to tell
I wasn't one to talk to strangers — No
don't say strangers
I was the befriended, too
shy to befriend them
It's hard to find strangers in a small town

I know what you mean, I said
Lisalore, from the Netherlands, taller than I, red
hair, cheek bones, narrow eyes
not as amazing as yours but was beautiful with
peach fuzz mustache
—that's a sacred document you're typing into—
She argued against there being a god
and played a duchess who fled Russia during
the revolution
We sang *Michelle* together at prom
I loved the last moments of the aristocracy right
before their country loses the war

Harpo's Veritable Forest

Taking on the act of
attention like it had
delineated form
independent of its objects

Always life getting in the way, dot dot
dot in ways so free of any and all
physical and virtual containers
If you make your voice bigger it does not make
you

Bigger. Pleasure of your own quiet presence is
from inevitable whisks from
your arms
The sly easing of your leg slipped into others'
who have already dismissed you for caking
them
with a violent—honk— cruel and dumb
smile of—honk—silence—ding!—honk—honk

You take your love where you get it

My analogous voice is pubescent: cuteness is
projected onto it

You take your love where you get it

If an arboretum is to be found
with all of its features identified,
in the most unassuming promenades,
each tree's branches slyly casting judgment
on their condition(s) and slipped through or around
wintery degrees of their nakedness
every nodal baboon's ass knot affecting curves
if they each, planted so still a cultivated
speech-like stance to endure,
will anyone climb it?

Pictures would come alive before blabbing
Are you or have you ever been a member of
what what?

Harpo Marx, naked crowned with roses
his wide veritable forest of harps
insists his mascot swan adapts to curdled milk

From by now ossified and grimacing suggested Venus.
You take your love where you get it.

This, the yield of your secrets, ah
in its grasp audire without searching
The Rapport Privilege images told

Post Pre-Rapport

This is after rapport is made, when
rapport is dirtier than *privilege*

You are something precious
whose instincts are foreign to us

We didn't have the patience
to watch the you gracefully fall
Our own movement mattered
to get to this table

*

anthropogenic problems such as pollution and
inequality as a ... no, don't interupt ... no, not a
collective responsibility,
a colect—what? No, not *invective response hillbilly*

*

Silver bullet, in feelings, *Einfühlung*
a kind of inner sympathy before
attempting to read a difficult poem.
Arm yourselves. Prepare for *basta*
Favorite game played in Spanish ... why the hurt
shrug? you're invited

*

Two elderly couples in line not quite cringing, not smirking
or winking a sense of surprise in their eyes to
each other up at the Library barista's expressing
in conversation with a woman his unconcealed
desire for tomorrow to be snowed out of a work
day

I watch as the couple get to the barista.
Pleasantries continue to my surprise

*

Pleasantries continue to my surprise

*

*I cast it with conviction, I cast it with
conviction* No, I cast it with conviction

Certainly — verily — partisan
in this group of many
its numerousness dwindles in
the message
stayed on by those who matter, hopefully.
I don't matter as much, having avoided

living in a city that sucks especially for the poor
having avoided being born black in a city that
sucks, especially for the black and poor
having avoided being born with female parts
having been queer in my own modest way

I cannot peddle my good self esteem for
anyone's benefit can I?
Can I benefit anyone's being for self esteem my
good peddling, I cannot
What does it mean to find the easiest way, no
not suicide, but still
not by depriving someone else of something?

The message stayed on

Those who matter and listen
The ear for melody helps, but
doesn't want music for music's sake

What does it want
What does it want?

A handful of billionaires
A handful of billions
A hand completely relaxed

A Hand Completely Relaxed, often ashamed
that ever wanted to learn how to live in the head
to become independent of the need to connect
meaningfully with others. Reassessment (for
other late adolescent positions as well) or
correction
      And honoring the original intention
of it.

A silver lining a silver bullet(--?)
You're it

Rapport Reprise

The Dillitante sewed patches
of replicas of *nir folx* code
Nir version of a toast
gets halted for a *bless it up*

Alone will find the pattern and break it
No gender neutral first person plural
you expect patience to understand starvation!

To try to share the dilettante's experience
Some have even credited it with
replacing museums — logically
Logically?
These homely drawings, poems and songs
embracing everyone within the privacy of

To try to share
the dilettante's experience, some
have even credited it with replacing museums
logically—Logically?
These homely drawings,
poems and songs embracing everyone
within the privacy of

To try to share the dilettante's
experience. Some have even, credited it
with replacing museums—logically. Logically?—
these homely drawings, poems and songs embrace
everyone within the privacy of

All the Sounds   Together Fine

the alphabet   habit
i   a sweater into the bath
you   your knee and it talk
the skin there   putty over rock
it   always   sincere, the same
when we   our teeth each one
an island up against
the water of our tongue—to   the letters
in the middle of it all symmetrical
all you to   a central calm
to   each   in emotion
I   my hand out to you
your life from the steam
we   our names to each other

Creed Shepard's poems have been published in *Smelt Money, Kaw Vally Independent, Beecher's, Hypocrite Reader* and more. He lives in Lawrence, Kansas and works various odd general labor jobs to supplement his part time job with the nonprofit Kansas Progress Institute where he runs communications, dabbles in fundraising to support his research assistance into the measuring of impacts on Kansas elections by the *Koch Brothers Complex*. He also runs Enduring Puberty Press, an earnestly unprofessional effort specializing in correspondence art, assemblages, epistolary form, in an effort to bypass literary, art and other elitist institutions to create new senses of community in which fiction, poetry, reviews, journalism, activism, and ideas can be shared. He blogs for Enduring Puberty Press at miuseofheterolinea.wordpress.com

This project was made possible, in part, by generous support from the Osage Arts Community.

Osage Arts Community provides temporary time, space and support for the creation of new artistic works in a retreat format, serving creative people of all kinds — visual artists, composers, poets, fiction and nonfiction writers. Located on a 152-acre farm in an isolated rural mountainside setting in Central Missouri and bordered by ¾ of a mile of the Gasconade River, OAC provides residencies to those working alone, as well as welcoming collaborative teams, offering living space and workspace in a country environment to emerging and mid-career artists. For more information, visit them at osageac.org

Osage Arts Community

www.ingramcontent.com/pod-product-compliance
Lightning Source LLC
Chambersburg PA
CBHW021450080526
44588CB00009B/783